MONEY. WEALTH. LIFE INSURANCE.

How the Wealthy Use Life Insurance as a Tax-Free
Personal Bank to Supercharge Their Savings

Jake Thompson

ISBN: 1494896478
ISBN-13: 978-1494896478

DEDICATION

To Alissa and Adri.

Contact Information

Jake Thompson
WealthbyJake.com
Jake@WealthbyJake.com

For a compilation of all the
references in this book or
to contact me, scan the
QR code or follow the link:

WealthbyJake.com/mwli1

ACKNOWLEDGMENTS

This book is a compilation of years of learning from some of the greatest people I know. Mentors, partners, and family have played a huge role in the completion of this book.

TABLE OF CONTENTS

CHAPTER 1

THE GREATEST TEST OF ALL

Travel with me in time for just a moment. It's the latter half of the 18th century, America has just gained independence from Britain, and the birth of a great nation is underway. At this time, several of the greatest minds in history are creating a legacy in what would become the modern United States.

Among many memorable events, one of the first financial tools of the western world is created. One with origins dating back to ancient Rome. And while no one knows it at this point, it will become a lifeline, a form of protection, and a champion of the greatest test of all...

...the test of time.

This tool will save thousands of individuals, families, and businesses from financial ruin and devastation for generations to come. It will be a beacon of hope amid chaos. And most importantly, it will be a source of stability and control in an industry full of crooks and criminals willing to do anything to make an extra buck.

Over the next few centuries, this tool will be so ingrained in American culture that making changes to it will be nearly impossible. It will become the last place truly protected from the corruption of greedy investors, untamed government, and unforeseen financial turmoil.

I like to refer to this tool as a personal bank on steroids, an unparalleled place to stockpile cash, and a financial bunker for tough times…

…but it is better known as cash value life insurance.

In this book, I'm going to show you why and how many wealthy American people, banks, and businesses have used life insurance as a platform to build wealth. I'm going to help you see why I've made it the foundation for every part of my finances and how you can do the same.

I'm also going to share how to create and use a specialized type of life insurance that I call "high cash value life insurance" and how to use it for your own and your loved ones' benefit. I'm going to teach you things only a small fraction of financial advisors and insurance agents have ever even heard of, much less understand. And finally, I'm going to share the raw numbers with you, the proof. Three case studies to illustrate exactly how everything works.

However, let's be clear. I'm not talking about the "garbage" peddled by most insurance agents. Rather, I'm talking about a highly efficient, supercharged savings vehicle designed to stockpile wealth. A product so powerful that it has been the cause of success for familiar names like Walt Disney, JC Penney, McDonald's, and many others. I'm talking about a vehicle designed by the wealthy to virtually guarantee financial success and amass wealth. More on that shortly…

Now, let's go back to history. For the following century and a half, America is booming. While we are young and ambitious, we are taking massive strides, firmly making our way into the pages of history.

Benjamin Franklin discovers electricity.

Thomas Edison invents the light bulb.

Alexander Bell invents the telephone.

At this point, we reach the Roaring Twenties, the decade that followed World War I. It is a time of wealth and excess, a time when people believe in the markets, the economy, and the government. But what soon follows would disrupt the lifestyle of almost every American. A series of truly tragic events. A time known as "The Great Depression."

The Great Depression

In October of 1929, the stock market suffered severe losses. It plunged over 22% in just a few days, making headlines across the country. Unfortunately, this was only the beginning.

Over the next several years, the markets would have difficulty recovering. The Dow Jones Industrial Average[1] would take a staggering 32-year setback, losing nearly 90% of its value.

After peaking at 381.17 in September 1929, it would close at a shocking 41.22 on July 8, 1932.[2]

---

[1] The Dow Jones Industrial Average (DJIA or "the Dow") represents 30 of the largest and most widely traded stocks in the United States. It includes companies like General Electric, Exxon and Microsoft and is one of the most watched indices in the world. It is an indicator of how the stock market is performing.

[2] "Historical Prices for Dow Jones Industrial Average." *Yahoo! Finance*. N.p., n.d. Web. 27 Dec.

Another 22 years would pass before it surpassed its all-time high previous to the crash of 1929.

Nearly 25% of Americans would be unemployed and unable to find work.[3] Over 40% of banks would shut down.[4] Millions of savings accounts would simply disappear. But here's where this story gets interesting.

While banks, businesses, and government sectors were closing their doors, one sector of the economy stood strong and steady, unaffected by these horrible circumstances. Life insurance companies.

Life insurance companies remained virtually unscathed. While the markets suffered severe losses, owners of cash value life insurance didn't lose a dime. They didn't lose any money in the Great Depression, and they haven't lost money since.

In fact, it was such a financially stable place that while many people lost everything, those who owned life insurance were paid profits in every single year of the Great Depression; a trend that continued every year after, even to the present.

This was truly a beacon of hope amid fear and chaos. It was the only place that triumphed over the devastation of that time.

The significance of this bit of history is relevant even in our generation.. Some people believe we have our most difficult times ahead. With complicated political issues at the door like the

2013. <http://finance.yahoo.com/q/hp?s=^DJI>.

[3] U.S. Bureau of the Census, Historical Statistics of the United States, Colonial Times to 1957 (Washington, D.C., 1960), p.70.

[4] "Great Depression." : *The Concise Encyclopedia of Economics*. N.p., n.d. Web. 28 Dec. 2013. <http://www.econlib.org/library/Enc/GreatDepression.html>.

national debt, government spending, Social Security, Medicare, and economic issues like inflation, taxes, debt, and so on, knowing how and where to keep your money safe is becoming increasingly important.

As you'll soon discover, life insurance companies played a big role in helping families and businesses stay afloat and ultimately trump these difficult circumstances.

JC Penney

When the market crashed in 1929, JC Penney, then a dry goods store for mining and farm families, was severely affected.

As its sole owner, James Cash Penney's company and personal wealth took a huge dive. The financial setbacks were so devastating that it even took a toll on his physical and mental health.

Fortunately, Mr. Penney had accumulated massive wealth inside his cash value life insurance policies and was able to borrow against them to help the company stay afloat and eventually bounce back. Cash value life insurance allowed him to keep his money safe and accessible and ultimately saved JC Penney from closing its doors.

When he died, the Grand Rapids Press wrote the following about Mr. Penney: "In the Great Stock Market Crash of 1929, he was almost wiped out, but with the money he borrowed on his $3 million dollar life insurance policy, he was able to rebound."[5]

Today, JC Penney takes in revenues of $18 billion a year and has over 1,100 stores worldwide.

---

[5] Alampur, Gopala. *Die Broke and Wealthy: The Insurance Bonanza That Beats the Tax Man While You're Still Alive.* Toronto: Chestnut Pub. Group, 2005. Print.

Walt Disney

Walt Disney is a name known by the vast majority of people across the globe; he was a man whose influence we still see today. From animated pictures, to theme parks and attractions, most of us have enjoyed his work..

What most people don't know is that without his cash value life insurance policies, much of what he built would not exist today.

Ever been to Disneyland? It is one of the most popular attractions on the planet. People fly in from all corners of the world to visit this magical kingdom.

But when Walt Disney wanted to take his successful animated features and television programs and turn them into an amusement park for children and parents, not everyone believed in his vision.

At the time, the only amusement parks in the country were run-down attractions. They were known to be untrustworthy and dirty, hardly a place for families and children. You might think of them more as a carnival in today's context.

Believing the idea would be unsuccessful, all potential financiers of Walt's venture rejected his request for financing. If Walt wanted to start his theme park, he'd have to find another way.

Fortunately, Walt was a very savvy individual, known for his success in business and finance, and had been stockpiling cash into his life insurance policies. Since banks and lenders continued to reject his financing needs, he decided to provide his own financing. As part of this, Walt borrowed against his cash value life insurance policies, and in 1955, Disneyland opened its doors for the first time. Within 1 year, over 3.5 million people visited the park. It was an instant success.

"It takes a lot of money to make these dreams come true. From the very start it was a problem. Getting the money to open Disneyland. About $17 million it took. And we had everything mortgaged, including my personal insurance..." – Walt Disney

McDonald's

All of us know McDonald's, the largest fast-food restaurant in the world, but not everyone knows Ray Kroc. Ray was one of three partners interested in opening a nationwide franchise of restaurants that sold hamburgers. After six years in business, Ray bought out the McDonald brothers and became the sole owner of the McDonald's we know today.

Ray relied heavily on cash value life insurance to store money, and this played a major role in getting the company off the ground.

For the first eight years, Ray didn't take a salary, and he took advantage of his two cash value life insurance policies to overcome constant cash flow problems. He used them to help cover the salaries of key employees, to pay for unforeseen expenses, and he even used some of the money to create an advertising campaign around the infamous Ronald McDonald.

Today, McDonald's serves more than 50 million people every day, with more than 30,000 locations around the world. Much of the success of McDonald's can be attributed to Ray's wise use of cash value life insurance.

Foster Farms

In 1939, a young couple named Max and Verda Foster borrowed against their life insurance policies to invest in an 80-acre farm in California where they could raise turkeys and chickens. Today, Foster Farms has more than 10,000 employees and sells products all across the globe.

Stanford University

After Leland and Jane Stanford lost their son to typhoid fever, they focused their efforts and wealth on helping other people.

In 1891, the first 555 students enrolled at Stanford University. But after Leland died in 1893, came financial struggles. Not wanting to give up what she so deeply believed in, Jane used her husband's life insurance policy proceeds to help fund operations and pay faculty, allowing Stanford University to weather a dangerous six-year period of financial distress.

Pampered Chef

After having success with Tupperware's marketing strategy, Doris Christopher believed women needed tools to help them make cooking quicker and easier. Using her cash value life insurance policy, Doris funded the first inventory for what is now a billion-dollar company with over 12 million customers, Pampered Chef.

Millions More

While we've only covered a few stories here, there is case after case of people that benefit from cash value life insurance daily. But individuals aren't the only ones taking advantage of its benefits. Banks and corporations are notorious for placing billions of dollars in cash value life insurance as well.

CHAPTER 2

BANKS, CORPORATIONS, AND
BILLIONS OF DOLLARS

While many wealthy individuals maximize the use of cash value life insurance, there is one specific group that shows true understanding of its value. This is the same sector that controls nearly every aspect of our economy. Banks.

Most of us can't really imagine the importance of the role that cash value life insurance plays in financial institutions, corporations, and banks. These organizations buy life insurance by the billions and use it for many different purposes. Not only does it increase their financial stability and reduce their taxes, it is also an ideal way to fund employee pensions, healthcare costs, and other benefits. It's so common among banks and corporations that it even has its own name. Bank-Owned Life Insurance (BOLI) and Corporate-Owned Life Insurance (COLI).

The FDIC makes available the balance sheets of nearly every major bank. The following figures are taken directly from

FDIC.gov[6] and represent the exact amount of money each bank holds in life insurance at the time of this book's publishing.

Bank	Life Insurance Assets
Bank of America	$19,607,000,000
Wells Fargo Bank	$17,739,000,000
JPMorgan Chase Bank	$10,327,000,000
U.S. Bank	$ 5,451,892,000

Banks are in the business of money. They employ some of the greatest minds in the world, including economists, attorneys, accountants, financial analysts, and other advisors, who help them increase the efficiency and use of their capital.

Banks place billions of dollars in life insurance for a reason. It's a reflection of the value they place on this powerful asset. For banks, life insurance provides the ultimate benefits in safety, stability, and growth. More importantly, the FDIC allows this asset to be classified as Tier 1 capital, which is the safest capital a bank can have.[7] Tier 1 capital is considered the core measure of a bank's financial strength.

We can learn a lot from banks, but they aren't the only ones who use this powerful asset to their advantage. Corporations are also heavily involved in buying life insurance in mass quantities.

The book *The Pirates of Manhattan* indicates that over 68% of

---

[6] "FDIC: Institution Directory." *FDIC: Institution Directory.* N.p., n.d. Web. 31 Dec. 2013.

[7] "RMS Manual of Examination Policies." *Federal Deposit Insurance Corporation*, n.d. Web. 2 Jan. 2014. <http://www.fdic.gov/regulations/safety/manual/section3-7.pdf>.

Fortune 1000 companies use life insurance to fund supplemental executive retirement plans (SERPs).[8] While businesses and corporations use it for many different purposes, it's interesting to note that one of them is the funding of employees' retirement plans. The ability to provide the stable growth necessary to create a predictable income is one of its most powerful features. As you'll soon discover, you too can use cash value life insurance to create a predictable income in the future as well.

Here is a list of some well-known companies that hold life insurance as an asset:[9]

---

[8] Dyke, Barry James. "CORPORATE-OWNED LIFE INSURANCE." *The Pirates of Manhattan: Systematically Plundering the American Consumer & How to Protect against It.* Portsmouth, NH: 555, 2007. 174-176. Print.

[9] Dyke, Barry James. "CORPORATE-OWNED LIFE INSURANCE." *The Pirates of Manhattan: Systematically Plundering the American Consumer & How to Protect against It.* Portsmouth, NH: 555, 2007. 174-176. Print.

Companies that Own Life Insurance

- General Electric
- Walt Disney
- Proctor & Gamble
- Crown Holdings
- AT&T
- Amway
- Nestle
- Panera Bread
- Prudential Insurance
- NetLife
- General Motors
- Harley Davidson
- H.J. Heinz
- International Paper
- Johnson & Johnson
- Lockheed Martin
- Lucent Technologies
- McGraw-Hill
- Norfolk Southern
- Outback SteakHouse
- Pfizer
- Pacific Gas & Electric
- Gannett Publishing
- Dow Chemical
- Lillian Vernon,
- Bed, Bath and Beyond
- Cendant
- CSX
- Monsanto
- BellSouth
- Office Depot
- Nike
- Starbucks
- United Healthcare
- Ryder Systems
- Anheuser-Busch
- Newell Rubbermaid
- KB Home
- Avon
- CVS
- Comcast
- United Technologies
- Verizon
- Wisconsin Energy

Lies on Wall Street

While banks and corporations are taking advantage of the benefits of cash value life insurance, the rest of America is falling victim to a deadly lie. We are being poisoned with the idea that volatile, risk-based investing in the stock market is the best way to prepare for retirement. We've been conned into believing that in order to achieve our goals, we must invest our hard earned money into the complex, misleading, unproven theories of Wall Street; that we must put our faith in large Wall Street firms to guess correctly how stocks will perform.

In the 1900s, it's estimated that over 50% of savings went into cash value life insurance. It was the staple for safety, protection, and predictable future income for many years. However, in the last few decades, people have fallen prey to a contrarian belief. By transitioning money from the safety and guarantees of a cash value life insurance policy to risk in the stock market, Wall Street firms stood to gain a lot. And they did. In fact, since the advent of the 401k and other government plans, the stock market has nearly quadrupled in total assets. This was a huge victory for Wall Street firms and advisors, but a significant loss for Americans.

Investment firms were a big part of the origin of government retirement plans. They positioned themselves to be the managers of the funds that ultimately made their way to these plans. What's worse is these companies don't participate in the same methods they pitch you and me every day.

I'm not going to go into the details of how investment firms have taken control of retirement funds, but suffice it to say, there has been a massive transition, for the worse, from safety and guarantees, to risky, unpredictable investments. Thousands of Americans are starting to see the outcomes of these failed models, and the consequences are devastating.

Now, to be clear, I'm not suggesting that stocks can't make

great investments. There is plenty of evidence to suggest they can, but wealthy investors like Warren Buffett and Charlie Munger aren't investing in stocks like most Americans and their financial advisors. Wealthy investors like Warren Buffett and Charlie Munger are far more careful with their wealth. Let me explain…

CHAPTER 3

How I Earned 300 Percent Returns

My family and I are just one of many examples of Americans who have enjoyed massive benefits in our finances thanks to cash value life insurance.

For nearly 11 years, I participated in the stock market and mutual funds like the average investor. In short, after over a decade, I had less money than I had put in. Like it might be with many of you, that strategy simply did not work for me.

Since that moment, I've followed a different philosophy. Never lose money. Almost every wealthy individual I've ever met or learned about was driven by keeping money safe, reducing risk, and making smart decisions. It's never uncalculated, and it's never out of their control.

In fact, one of the greatest investors of our day, Warren Buffett, subscribes to a similar mentality. When it comes to investing, he's quoted as saying, "Rule number one is never lose money. Rule number two is never forget rule number one."

If you watch the TV series "Shark Tank" for 5 minutes, you'll understand how the wealthy look at risk. These billionaire investors pass up opportunity after opportunity waiting for home run deals. I call the risk they take "smart risk," and I'll explain why later.

In 2008, the markets took another huge dive. It's common for the market to have massive setbacks, but this one was devastating. Some have said it was the worst since the Great Depression.

While everyone was in a panic, I had not lost a penny. I had my money safely tucked away inside my cash value life insurance policies. I was safely growing my money, unaffected by the changes in the markets.

As an increasing number of people struggled with losses, more opportunities emerged for those of us that had access to money.

After waiting patiently, I found the perfect opportunity to invest in two real estate properties. Just like many of the people in the stories I've shared, I borrowed from my cash value policies and paid for the properties in full. I purchased them for the same price they sold for in 1984, nearly 25 years earlier.

Now, fast forward 3 years. Those properties have more than tripled in value, and I've recouped my entire investment from rental income alone. A handsome reward for patience and smart, calculated risk taking.

I stuck by my rule: never lose money. While that can't always be guaranteed, the absolute worst case scenario I could think of was breaking even on my investment. There was a lot of upside potential and seemingly little downside. It was a risk worth taking.

I consider myself very fortunate to have learned about cash value life insurance and to have made it such an important part of my life. I've been blessed to avoid so many of the pitfalls and disasters that plague the vast majority of hard working Americans. Greed has shaped the investment community, rigging the game against the individual investor (you and me). I've witnessed this first hand. As pretty a picture as they have painted, the financial industry is unraveling quickly, and people experiencing the market roller coaster are looking for a better way to handle their finances. I urge you to seriously consider what I'm about to teach you, and to think about how you can adapt these principles into your finances.

CHAPTER 4

WINNING WITH TAXES

I'm constantly amazed at how most people plan for taxes. The way the majority of Americans handle their taxes greatly differs from how the wealthy handle theirs. While most Americans dump money into qualified plans for "tax savings" the wealthy aren't willing to let Uncle Sam decide the best time and rate to pay taxes.

This is what I like to call the "401k predicament."

The fact is that retirement plans like 401ks, IRAs, and other government plans are designed to postpone the taxes you will pay on your earned income.

If you are in a higher tax bracket today than when you take your money out, you will save money on taxes (you win). If, on the other hand, you are in a lower tax bracket today than when you take it out, you'll pay more taxes (you lose). So, the predicament becomes whether or not to postpone taxes. In reality, it's not that much of a predicament because the evidence is overwhelming. Most people are clearly in a higher tax bracket at retirement than during their working years. They are losing the tax game.

In the late 70s and early 80s, when retirement plans like the 401k started, tax brackets were extremely high and designed to be lower in retirement years. Even though this concept worked then, it just doesn't work now.

I took the time to interview 5 Certified Public Accountants to find out what they see every day as it relates to retirees and tax brackets. I was stunned by the confidence in their answers.

Here are a few of their comments:

"I'm seeing them retire with very few deductions, and if they've been socking it away in 401ks or just tax deferred plans, I see them retiring with very few deductions and 100% taxable income." - Kevin CPA

"I see it all the time with people who've created wealth and done the right things with their money throughout their life. By the time they retire, they're actually making more money than they did when they were working." - Cameron CPA

"I think that most folks expect a lower tax bracket and that doesn't develop the way they anticipate - Rick CPA

Listen to the full interviews by scanning the QR code or following this link:

WealthbyJake.com/mwli1

The majority of Americans are socking money into retirement plans that postpone taxes; this is a poor bet. Across the board, people are retiring with more income and lower deductions. That combination erodes their retirement funds. Here's why.

During your working years, you have a lot of elements that can potentially keep your tax bracket down. The mortgage interest deduction, student loan interest deduction, exemptions for children, and lower income in the earlier stages of your career.

Inflation alone is likely to bump you into higher tax brackets, but this is especially true when you take away deductions and exemptions, leaving nothing to offset increased income. This is exactly what our CPAs are seeing for many Americans. And the more successful you have been, the more you lose.

Last but not least, it's clear that the government needs, and is seeking, more revenue. The combination of high spending, high national debt, and some of the lowest tax brackets in history could be a possible indicator of increasing taxes. And as of right now, some of those increases have already taken place.

While I hesitate to make a blanket statement here, knowing every situation is unique, consider the benefits of retiring tax-free. There is peace in not having to worry about what tax bracket the future holds. Chances are you'll not only save on taxes, but you'll also sleep better at night.

The truth is, more and more people are having the proverbial light-bulb-over-the-head moment. They've realized that taxes aren't going down, and they need to rethink their tax plan.

That's why a tax-free retirement is a breath of fresh air.

Chapter 5

What the Wealthy Know About Risk

Discussion of risk is common in the financial industry. It's widely accepted that risk is a natural part of building wealth. While I agree that taking the right kind of risk can, at times, be extremely profitable, I do not believe it is a requirement, and I certainly don't believe it should be taken lightly.

There are two types of risk. The first one has the potential for creating significant wealth. It's the type that Walt Disney took when he started Disneyland, the type that Ray Kroc took when he started McDonald's, and it's the type thousands of men and women have taken throughout history to achieve their dreams. I call it "smart risk."

Smart risk is simple. It's calculated. You understand why you are taking it, and you see the potential gains for risk well taken. This doesn't always go your way, but that's okay, you know what you are in for when you take it.

The other type of risk is an excuse to make unsound financial decisions. It's justification for a bad investment model. It's the kind of risk Wall Street tells us is necessary. I call it "dumb risk."

Dumb risk is uncalculated, you don't know why you're taking it, other than because you are told "there is no reward without risk."

Now you tell me, is it smart risk or dumb risk to invest money without knowing where it goes, why it's going there, or what you'll gain from it? Most Americans are taking a dumb risk, unnecessarily riding the Wall Street roller coaster.

On the other hand, taking smart risks is an advanced skill. Not everyone wants or even needs to take risks. If it's not a smart risk, don't take it. Most people would do just fine saving faithfully and growing their money in a conservative tax-free environment like life insurance. No risk necessary. This is why so many corporations use this strategy to pay employee pensions. It's safe, and they know they can count on it. No risk necessary.

Let me give you a great example of smart risk versus dumb risk. Warren Buffett makes billions of dollars buying stocks. Millions of Americans invest in the stock market every day. While they both buy stocks, their situations are extremely different. For Mr. Buffett, buying a stock is buying a company. He knows the company; he calculates the risk, sees the potential, and pulls the trigger only if the value he sees is more than the investment he makes. The vast majority of Americans are mindlessly tossing money into the market, hoping something good will come from it. One is smart risk, the other is dumb risk.

CHAPTER 6

SUPERCHARGED SAVINGS WITH CASH VALUE LIFE INSURANCE

A few years ago, I was approached by an older gentleman in his early sixties named Jim. Jim wanted my help and expertise to move more assets into a high cash value life insurance policy.

When I asked him why he was looking to purchase more life insurance, he told me an interesting story. Twenty-four years ago, Jim was approached by his brother Scott, a newly licensed insurance agent, to buy an insurance policy for him and his family. As you can imagine, he felt obligated to buy the policy. His fear of telling his brother "no" was far greater than the few hundred dollars a month that the policy would cost him. There's a good chance a few of you have experienced this same situation.

As the years went on, his investment strategy was to follow the advice of the "experts" and his peers... "Invest in stocks, mutual funds, and your 401k." The same advice most Americans hear daily.

Now, fast-forward 24 years. Jim has assets in 401ks, IRAs, and his life insurance policy. However, the interesting part is that it took Jim 24 years to realize his life insurance policy was his best investment. It had earned a little over 6%; it never lost money, and it had outperformed the investments in his 401k and IRAs. Now, he wanted to move the rest of his money into a high cash value life insurance policy.

Ironically, the policy he had so reluctantly purchased from his brother turned out to be the smartest financial decision of his life.

This is not an uncommon story. I've heard it more than once. Had my client been presented with a high cash value life insurance policy, as opposed to a more traditional type, he would have seen the benefits he was excited about much sooner.

Growth

A case study by Mass Mutual Life Insurance Company showed the performance of 3 policies from 1980 to 2013. The internal rate of return for each of these policies was 5.65%, 6.02%, and 6.22%.[10]

Download the MassMutual Case Study. Scan the QR code or follow the link:

WealthbyJake.com/mwli2

And while that is not necessarily an excessive return, it's better

---

[10] Historical Dividend Studies From Massachusetts Mutual Life Insurance Company. N.p.: Massachusetts Mutual Life Insurance, n.d. 2008. Web. 23 Dec. 2013. < https://fieldnet.massmutual.com/public/life/pdfs/li7954.pdf>.

than what most people have earned in the last decade or two in the markets, without the emotional stress that comes with such a wicked roller coaster ride.

According to Crestmont Research, the S&P 500 earned actual returns (before management fees and taxes) of 0% in the last 5 years and of 2% in the last 10 years. You have to go back 20 years to hit a high of 7% annual returns.[11]

Download the Crestmont Research Study. Scan the QR code or follow the link:

WealthbyJake.com/mwli3

Mutual funds prove to be even worse. According to Standard & Poor's, over 99% of mutual funds consistently underperform the S&P 500. Chances are, if you've invested in the stock market and/or mutual funds, the S&P 500 returns would be your best case scenario.

In comparison, cash value life insurance has done very well, and we've only started scratching the surface.Cash value life insurance is one of the most tax-friendly financial tools available. Money inside cash value life insurance, when handled properly, grows tax-free, can be used tax-free, and passes on tax- free.

So, let's consider 2 additional factors: taxes and fees.

---

[11] 2012 CRESTMONT RESEARCH STOCK MARKET MATRIX. N.p.: n.p., n.d. Crestmont Research. Www.CrestmontResearch.com, 2013. Web. 23 Dec. 2013. <http://www.crestmontresearch.com/docs/Stock-Matrix-Tax-Exempt-Nominal4-11x17.pdf>.

The case study showed life insurance policy returns of 6%. If you are in a 30 percent tax bracket, this is the equivalent of 8.6% returns with taxes.

Now, assuming a conservative 1% management fee, the equivalent return in the market would have to be upwards of 9.6% to compare to the life insurance returns. I can safely say (with the research to back it) that it's not exactly realistic to expect 10% returns every year in the market. Anyone who has had money in the markets for more than a few years knows that.

We could also calculate the additional cost of term insurance you would have to buy in order to compare more accurately to what the cash value policy offers. While we are heavily focusing on this as a place to stockpile cash, it's important to remember that the death benefit it provides is extremely advantageous as well. We'd have to increase our "equivalent returns" even higher to account for that benefit.

In short, the growth inside a cash value life insurance policy is not flashy, but it's conservative, consistent, and extremely competitive. Anyone who tells you otherwise is woefully ill-informed.

"But I Can Get A Better Return"
You might think the point of this section is to try and convince you that you can't get better returns, but it's not.

I strongly believe that the results of conventional forms of investing, especially stocks and mutual funds, fall short of what a solid cash value policy has to offer, with far less risk. But truthfully, it doesn't matter.

One of the best benefits of cash value life insurance is the guaranteed access to money anytime you want it. If you believe you can get better returns somewhere else, and you're willing to take the risk, the insurance policy will actually make the investment more profitable. More on how that works later.

Case and point. I have money in life insurance, but I've leveraged my policies for greater growth opportunities. My real estate investments have paid double-digit returns consistently for several years, and my policies have not restricted me from making those investments. On the contrary, accessing those dollars from my policies has simply made my investments more profitable.

Look at it this way: Your policy is creating a benchmark to help you decide if a risk is worth taking. If your policy is earning 5%, that is your benchmark. If you can do better than 5%, the money is there for you to use and increase your returns elsewhere, so long as you are willing to take the risk.

In some cases, because the money inside a cash value life insurance policy is so safe, you can use external sources of capital, like a third party bank, with your life insurance as collateral, to borrow capital. Often this money can be cheaper than the cost of capital from the insurance company, offering you additional value through borrowing at a cost of capital lower than the growth of the policy.

Tax-Free Growth

I don't know about you, but I'm worried about taxes. Most people give up more on income taxes than almost anything else, and, as we've seen, this can really damage your finances. I know that if I don't prepare adequately, I'll have to suffer the consequences.

I believe one of the most attractive benefits of cash value life insurance is the way it is taxed. This alone attracts those that want protection from the uncertainty of taxes.

Let's talk about a few of those tax benefits.

The first, and arguably one of the most important, is tax-free growth.

It's actually pretty simple. Growth inside an insurance policy is called a dividend and, by definition, is considered a "return of premium." Since it is considered a return of what you have already paid, it is not taxable.

That being said, there is one caveat: As the policy grows, you will have undoubtedly accumulated more than you contributed if you've designed it for high cash value. If at any point you decide to withdraw your money from the insurance policy, the growth (everything above the cost basis of the policy) can be taxable.

For example, if I've contributed $100,000 to the policy, and my cash value is $300,000, withdrawals up to $100,000 would be considered cost basis and would not be taxable. However, withdrawals past that cost basis would result in taxation. Handling this policy correctly means I can avoid the taxable events by using a combination of withdrawals and loans. I'll talk more about how to do this later.

As long as it remains intact, the policy will continue to grow tax-free indefinitely. As you'll soon discover, there is practically no reason to ever cancel this policy, keeping those dollars tax-free for the rest of your life.

The appeal of tax-free growth on your money is one of the biggest reasons large organizations and savvy individuals plug millions of dollars into these policies every year. You'll have a hard time finding these types of tax benefits elsewhere.

Tax-Free Death Benefit

When you've amassed a large amount of wealth like Walt Disney, JC Penney, Ray Kroc, and others, there's only one thing that stands in the way of passing that hard work on to your family. The government.

Whether you have a big estate or a small estate, passing on money can be painful. Some of the largest estates are stripped to nearly nothing after taxes and probate.

One example is that of the King of Rock and Roll himself, Elvis Presley. At the time of his death in 1977, Presley's estate was worth $10 million. 73 percent of the value of the estate went toward legal fees, estate administration costs, and estate taxes, leaving only roughly $3 million to his daughter.

In addition to tax-free growth, cash value life insurance provides a tax-free death benefit and one that bypasses probate altogether.

This means your life insurance death benefit will transfer with no income tax to those you leave it to, and there won't be fees and expenses required for that to happen.

One thing I can guarantee, there is no better asset to die with than life insurance. It is the most heavily used estate planning tool in the country because it can help assure your family gets more of your hard-earned money, and the government gets less.

Social Security

This is the icing on the cake in the tax discussion.

As taxpayers, we all pay a social security tax. Its purpose is to give us an income down the road when we retire, but there is one problem...

Most people don't plan to have social security as their primary source of income, so if you've been diligent in saving and want to take a retirement income down the road from money you've saved or invested, your social security income could be at risk of taxation.

However, since it was originally a tax paid to receive it, it seems a little unfair to pay a tax on it. In other words, being penalized for having saved well.

The perk of cash value life insurance is that it remains one of the last places from which you can draw money and not have it count against this social security tax. Even other tax-free sources of income, like tax-free bonds, still count as income in the social security tax equation.

Cash value life insurance offers the best tax benefits across the board.

Guarantees
Cash value life insurance policies are also equipped with solid guarantees.

While dividends, or company profits, are technically not guaranteed, a portion of the growth inside your policy is.

In the event that the insurance company can't pay out a dividend, you are guaranteed to see an increase in your cash value inside your policy. This means you'll always move forward.

While the above is true, it's also important to know that the insurance companies I personally recommend have paid profits for over 100 years straight, making it pretty unlikely that they won't continue to do so in the future.

Accessing Money Inside Your Policy

While it's already been mentioned in a few sections, I want to go into more detail on the best ways to use the money from your cash value life insurance policy.

First and foremost, as you build cash value in your policy, you can access those funds at any time and for any reason. There are two ways to do so.

Withdrawals

One option to access money from your policy is to actually withdraw it. It is possible, but I don't typically recommend it. The second option, loans, can provide more advantages and better benefits.

Loans

The fundamental difference between a loan and a withdrawal is that the withdrawal comes from your money, while the loan comes from the insurance company.

By contract, the insurance company guarantees you the ability to borrow money up to the amount you have in cash value. Since you are a policyholder, these loans come at competitive rates.[12] Why? Because you have collateralized the loan with your cash value, and there is no risk to the insurance company.

That low risk and low maintenance use of money is a great way for the insurance company to safely grow its capital, so they offer it to you at very advantageous rates.

For example, a company I have policies with just paid a 7.1% dividend last year, and their loan rate was 5%. Borrowing from the insurance company in that scenario netted me the difference.

---

[12] Not all insurance companies have the same loan provisions and may not provide the same benefits.

Beyond the simple differences in loan rates and dividends, there are other advantages to loans over withdrawals.

When you decide to opt for a loan, there are no tax consequences if you borrow beyond your cost basis (what you've put in). On the other hand, withdrawing past your cost basis could incur taxes. In addition to being tax friendly, a loan keeps the policy cash value growing and working for you; it keeps the death benefit high, and it makes you accountable for the money you use.

By borrowing money from the insurance company, you ensure that your capital never stops compounding. It forces you to keep that capital constantly working in your favor.

The Safest Place on the Planet

At the beginning of this book, we walked through the time of The Great Depression. A very difficult time indeed.

But amid such chaos and confusion, life insurance companies held strong. While there is never a guarantee that something won't happen, based on its track record, it's possible to deduct that cash value life insurance is the best bet for safety of capital. That's the exact reason that banks rely so heavily on it.

These policies are extremely well-oiled machines, and it would be very hard to take them down. We've seen them consistently providing growth for over a century while experiencing twelve recessions and one Great Depression.

Stock Companies vs. Mutual Companies

There are two different kinds of life insurance companies: stock and mutual.

Stock companies pay out earnings to stockholders first, then potentially to policyholders.

Mutual companies, on the other hand, have no shareholders and only pay out earnings to their policyholders. The profits are what we refer to as dividends.

I like to compare this dynamic to making a deposit at the bank, and that deposit giving me credit as a shareholder to receive company profits. A highly unlikely scenario at a bank but a good example of how a mutual company operates.

Based on all this information, a stock company does not stand out as the best way to maximize the use of cash value life insurance. Mutual companies provide the most benefit and are clearly a better option.

No Minimums or Maximums

There is no government minimum or maximum contribution to a cash value life insurance policy. We are free to contribute as much or as little as we want.[13] The only limitation will be how much insurance the insurance company is willing to offer. More on that shortly.

---

[13] If the cumulative premium payments exceed certain rules under the Internal Revenue Code, the life insurance policy may become a Modified Endowment Contract (MEC). This may alter the tax status of the policy. A professional well-versed in these products can ensure the policy does not become a MEC.

Extreme Flexibility

When talking about cash value life insurance, most people are under the impression that premiums are due every month or year for nearly the rest of their life. This is hardly the case with high cash value life insurance.

One of the benefits of high cash value life insurance is the amount of money front loaded into the policy. Because we jam-pack these policies with high levels of cash in the beginning years, we create a large amount of flexibility to adjust to different circumstances.

Future premiums can be reduced or even completely eliminated in any year if necessary.

This gives the policyholder the ability to make a plan today and adjust, if necessary, tomorrow.

Keep in mind this is not your run of the mill policy, it's specially designed for these benefits. I've designed 3 specific case studies that will show you some of the flexibility discussed here. We'll look at those shortly.

Death Benefit

While I have mentioned the tax benefits surrounding the death benefit, I want to go into this topic more in depth.

First, it's important to note that the risk of your death is now on the insurance company's shoulders, in addition to the fact that you have insurance. This is critical to caring financially for yourself and your loved ones.

Secondly, if your money is growing safely, while simultaneously giving you life insurance, you are saving yourself an added cost to insure your family, and you are accelerating the wealth your family accumulates at the time of your death.

The death benefit is a great side benefit of these cash value policies and can be the jump-start to future wealth within your family. You'll almost accidentally pass on a significant amount of money to your loved ones.

Another factor to account for is the ever-increasing amount of death benefit. As cash value builds inside your policy, there is a natural increase in the death benefit. The more cash value you put into the policy, the higher the death benefit goes. Therefore, the older you get, the more money you will pass on to your family naturally. Pretty cool, right?

The "High" in High Cash Value Life Insurance

I wanted to make sure I included a section that distinguished why I call it "high" cash value life insurance because it's different from your traditional policy.

Have you ever heard of Joe Ayoob? This guy holds the world record for flying a paper airplane: 226 ft. 10 inches. That's a little over 3 quarters of a football field. It's pretty crazy...

While you could give me the exact same piece of paper Joe Ayoob uses to fly world-record paper airplanes, there's really no chance I'll be able to fold it for high performance. Mine barely makes it across the table, let alone a football field. The same concept applies here. The performance of a cash value life insurance policy is based on how it's structured (or folded).

For example, a typical cash value life insurance policy has a big fat $0 of cash value in the first year or even in the first several years. It can take decades to perform, which is the main reason some people don't like it. While eventually it does recoup those early years and performs well, it's not the most efficient.

A high cash value life insurance policy is much more efficient, as it focuses on reducing the cost of insurance inside the policy and putting more of your dollars into cash value. As a result, we see positive returns in the first few years, meaning more cash value than contributions, and better performance every year moving forward. That design is like folding the paper airplane. It may be the same product the insurance company offers, but without the design for high cash value, it doesn't produce the same benefit.

Ownership

I'd like to add one small nugget here. Since the primary focus is not the death benefit in many cases, the insured (the person whose life is insured) is not the top priority. You can maintain complete control as the owner of a policy while insuring someone else's life. The insured is simply the life the insurance is based on but that person has no say in policy decisions.

So if health, age, or other factors don't allow you to get the insurance you need, you can simply own the insurance on the life of another individual.

Closing a Policy

Life insurance policies can be closed at any time. Your cash value is also called your "surrender value." You can walk away with your surrender value whenever you want. However, if you do choose to close your policy, you will be required to pay taxes on the growth of that policy (anything above what you have contributed).

This is the main reason to maintain an intact policy until death. With a little planning, you can have the guarantee that your family will always be left with more money than the amount you would get if you cashed out thanks to the death benefit.

With proper handling, you can exercise options inside any insurance policy to eliminate future premiums, or out of pocket payments, and simply let your cash value grow. This is referred to as a "reduced paid up" policy.

You can still access the cash value while the policy remains in force. This keeps your money working inside the policy, maintaining all the powerful advantages, without having to make additional contributions.

CHAPTER 7

A MORE EFFICIENT SAVINGS STRATEGY

Cash value life insurance solves a lot of problems that we've already discussed. However, in this chapter, I want to discuss a few other areas where it can save you, and earn you, additional money.

Throughout your life, you'll likely save hundreds of thousands of dollars to buy all kinds of necessary and unnecessary items. Cars, homes, medical expenses, education, weddings, to name a few.

It's clear that borrowing on high-interest credit cards and loans is an expensive way to pay for those items, so I won't go into any more detail on that topic. I'm going to assume you save and pay cash.

In addition to large purchases, you're hopefully keeping emergency savings liquid, safe, and accessible.

What most people haven't thought about, however, are the thousands of dollars that have been lost (or not earned) by saving for these items in the conventional way.

When you pay cash for something, you have to save for it first. And where do you save this cash? Somewhere you know you can get it when you need it. For most people, this is some form of savings or checking account.

There are two problems with this practice. The first is in regards to how you save and the second, how you spend.

As you set money aside for these large purchases and emergencies, you're putting thousands of dollars to very little use in low interest, taxable accounts. If you're earning 1% inside a savings account but could be earning 5% in a life insurance policy, you're missing out on 4% interest every year. This is called opportunity cost, and it means thousands of dollars lost in your lifetime.

In addition to low interest and growth, you are also required to pay taxes on what little you have earned. This reduces your savings efficiency even further.

However, this doesn't only apply to large purchases. You may keep cash for emergency savings. You might be an investor or business owner that sits on large amounts of cash, waiting to use it.

When you plug cash value life insurance into the equation, your savings dollars earn more, and your tax burden is reduced. It's a much more efficient way to save.

Now the second problem. When you pay cash for a car, you typically don't plan to put that money back into your savings on any schedule. You simply plan for your next purchase and save what's necessary to make it. This emphasizes the real value you are placing on your dollars, which is very little.

Let me explain…

When you borrow money from a bank, do you expect them to charge you interest? Of course. When you lend someone money, do you expect them to pay you interest? Of course. Yet, when you use your own money, you place no such value there. Why?

This is exactly why I recommend taking loans against the insurance policy. It ensures that you are accountable to the money you use. It ensures you never liquidate your account to make a purchase with no intention of keeping that money growing. It requires you to never interrupt the compound growth of your dollars. Overall, it makes you more accountable, more efficient, and more profitable.

Making Your Investments Better

As I've previously mentioned, using your policy to make investments only makes those investments more profitable. I'm going to address why.

Let's jump into an example. Let's say I've got an investment where I can earn 10% returns, and I invest $100,000.

At the end of the year, I'll have made $10,000. At capital gain rates of 15%, I'll owe $1,500 in taxes.

Total profit: $8,500

Now, let's assume I've got that money tucked in my cash value life insurance policies, and I borrow the money from the insurance company at 5%. Here's how it breaks down:

Investment Returns	$10,000
Policy Returns* (Tax Free)	$5,000
Policy Interest (Tax Deductible)	($5,000)
Taxes	($750)
Total Profit	**$9,250**

*Assumes 5%

Essentially, what we've done is turn an effective 8.5% return into a 9.25% return. How? By taking advantage of an interest deduction that reduced my taxable gain to $5,000.

However, this is a very simple version of the story. What we haven't mentioned is that the money in my life insurance policy is giving me the death benefit and is growing competitively after the investment is liquidated. Without the policy, my money would most likely go back to being extremely inefficient, in a low-interest, taxable environment.

All this proves that life insurance makes you smarter as an investor. It makes your investments more profitable and gives you a benchmark to beat. If you can do better than the policy growth, do it. If you can't, don't. It's that simple.

Making Your Business Better
Just like investments, cash value life insurance can add extra benefits to what you are already doing in your business. Why? It keeps your money working more efficiently and helps reduce the business' taxable income.

By using this type of policy, business owners are able to make better use of their capital, reduce their personal and business tax liability, cover key employees in a more efficient way, and a slew of other items depending on the business.

CASE STUDY 1

CONSISTENT CONTRIBUTIONS

In this case study, I will illustrate the exact layout of a high cash value life insurance policy. I'm going to show you the following :

- Annual contribution of $20,000 per year
- Total cash value at the end of every year
- Total death benefit at the end of every year
- Future income from the policy

Keep in mind that these are examples, but a similar ratio of contributions to cash value should still apply no matter how little or how much you put in, and mostly similar regardless of your age or gender. $20,000 is not a magic number, a limit, or a minimum of any kind. There are no minimums or maximums as stated previously.

Year	Age End Year	Annual Outlay Beg Year	Net Cash Value End Year	Net Death Benefit End Year
		40 Year Old Male, Good Health, Non-Smoker		
1	41	20,000	18,365	951,544
2	42	20,000	38,520	970,298
3	43	20,000	59,491	1,003,148
4	44	20,000	80,899	1,034,194
5	45	20,000	102,752	1,063,707
6	46	20,000	123,990	1,088,280
7	47	20,000	146,486	1,114,154
8	48	20,000	170,333	1,141,433
9	49	20,000	195,619	1,169,739
10	50	20,000	222,409	1,199,103
11	51	20,000	250,770	1,229,586
12	52	20,000	280,730	1,261,207
13	53	20,000	312,411	1,294,234
14	54	20,000	345,877	1,328,719
15	55	20,000	381,258	1,364,941
16	56	20,000	419,434	1,404,916
17	57	20,000	460,514	1,448,531
18	58	20,000	504,725	1,495,915
19	59	20,000	552,203	1,546,595
20	60	20,000	603,109	1,600,625
21	61	20,000	657,336	1,656,604
22	62	20,000	714,570	1,714,916
23	63	20,000	774,917	1,775,824
24	64	20,000	838,493	1,839,481
25	65	20,000	905,461	1,905,902
26	66	20,000	975,910	1,974,974
27	67	20,000	1,050,087	2,046,781
28	68	20,000	1,128,142	2,121,084
29	69	20,000	1,210,266	2,198,013

What you'll quickly notice as you review the first year of this illustration is that you're actually behind. You've put in $20,000 but only have $18,365. While better than the typical $0 in the first year of most cash value policies, it's still behind. But this is a small price to pay, and it has a minimal effect on policy growth. Here's why...

Since this is not a savings account, we are abiding by a different set of rules. The insurance company is taking on a lot of risk. In this scenario, they're letting you use the majority of your money and taking on the risk of nearly 1 million dollars in the event that you die (Death Benefit year 1: $951,544). In order to do so, they hold a little money upfront, and every year you have the policy, a little more of it comes back. In only a few short years, you are back in the positive. This ensures the insurance company is still protected, and you get maximum benefits.

Now, let's jump to year 29 in this illustration. The cash value is $1,210,266 at this point and growing at a 5% internal rate of return (meaning as if every year your money earned 5%). So even though you were slightly behind in the early years, it's had little to no effect on future growth. Here's the kicker though; you now have $2,198,013 of death benefit, an extra $987,747 going to your loved ones if you died that year. You've successfully built in a massive legacy that will have a significant effect on your family.

So here's the question. Are you willing to give up the use (emphasis on 'use') of some of those early dollars (with minimal long term effect on growth) in exchange for the ability to pass nearly an extra million dollars to your loved ones? Are you willing to give up the use of a few dollars in exchange for tax-free growth, access to your money, guarantees, safety, and a slew of other benefits we've already discussed?

For most of us that's a pretty simple question to answer.

Future Income
Now that we've looked at the years of savings, let's look at the second half of the numbers.

Keep in mind, at this point, we have saved a total of $580,000.

			Net	Net
	Age	Annual	Cash	Death
	End	Outlay	Value	Benefit
Year	Year	Beg Year	End Year	End Year

40 Year Old Male, Good Health, Non-Smoker

Year	Age End Year	Annual Outlay Beg Year	Net Cash Value End Year	Net Death Benefit End Year
30	70	0	1,275,767	2,068,296
31	71	0	1,344,626	2,129,291
32	72	0	1,416,924	2,192,600
33	73	0	1,492,833	2,259,028
34	74	0	1,572,548	2,328,528
35	75	0	1,656,142	2,400,971
36	76	-120,000	1,617,371	2,296,945
37	77	-120,000	1,576,017	2,193,757
38	78	-120,000	1,532,041	2,091,467
39	79	-120,000	1,485,415	2,011,645
40	80	-120,000	1,435,951	1,934,522
41	81	-120,000	1,383,567	1,855,245
42	82	-120,000	1,328,055	1,773,840
43	83	-120,000	1,269,113	1,701,539
44	84	-120,000	1,206,436	1,627,740
45	85	-120,000	1,139,687	1,549,581
46	86	-120,000	1,068,697	1,467,175
47	87	-120,000	993,127	1,380,400
48	88	-120,000	912,160	1,288,456
49	89	-120,000	825,251	1,190,840
50	90	-120,000	731,811	1,086,958
51	91	-120,000	631,323	976,181
52	92	-120,000	523,532	857,210
53	93	-120,000	408,036	729,208
54	94	-120,000	284,612	591,219
55	95	0	279,204	568,137
56	96	0	272,505	538,856
57	97	0	266,912	501,482
58	98	0	265,520	453,306
59	99	0	274,114	389,863

This is the second half of the example above. At age 70, we've decided to stop putting money into the policy, and by age 76, we've decided to take income from the policy.

In this scenario, we are successfully taking $120,000 per year for 19 years. A total of $2,280,000 of total income. Not bad.

Now keep in mind that this income is tax-free when handled properly and doesn't have to be taken out in systematic increments. You can take it out however you see fit. It's recommended that you consult with a professional to make sure it's done correctly.

Summary

Case Study 1: Consistent Contributions	
Total Contributions	$580,000
Total Income	$2,280,000

Tip of the Iceberg

I've prepared 2 more case studies that show a different way to fund a cash value life insurance policy, but before I go into them, I want to emphasize some important points.

These illustrations represent exactly how your money would grow inside a well-designed, high cash value life insurance policy. But truthfully, this is just the tip of the iceberg.

What the numbers can't show are numerous reasons this type of strategy is highly valuable, and heavily used by America's wealthiest individuals and families. Here's a brief list of the items the numbers can't show:

1. The extra growth earned by not using a low interest savings account to save money for large purchases (i.e. cars, boats, down payments, weddings, education).
2. The taxes you saved by keeping your growth tax-free.
3. The losses you would avoid by keeping it safe.

4. The interest you would save by having access to your money and not being required to borrow from credit card companies, banks, and other lending institutions at high rates.
5. The extra interest you could earn by using your dollars for investments or business opportunities.

All these items have been discussed in previous chapters, so reference them as needed.

What's important to note is that there is a completely different set of numbers that go hand in hand with the simple projection of growth. The savings in interest, taxes, and opportunity cost amount to thousands and thousands of additional dollars that contribute to your future wealth.

The "Banking" Concepts

We've already covered loans (See 'Accessing Money Inside Your Policy'), but this case study helps illustrate a very important point. There are entire financial philosophies geared specifically toward this idea, some call it Infinite Banking, Privatized Banking, Becoming Your Own Banker, etc. Much of this philosophy stems from Nelson Nash's book *Becoming Your Own Banker*. I'm going to simplify it for you.

This refers to the idea that you should treat your capital in the same way whether you use it or let someone else use it. Let's look back at year 29. There is $1,210,266 of cash value. That's a significant amount of money. Since the insurance company is doing its part to grow the money, there is really only one reason for possibly falling short of it... you. If you take money from it and don't put it back, you'll be single handedly responsible for not reaching your financial potential. Don't let yourself be that reason.

Apart from the fact that loans are advantageous, they keep the death benefit high and tax-friendly; loans ensure that your money never stops growing. Every dollar inside the policy is virtually guaranteed to reach its potential because it grows uninterrupted. It puts you at a higher level of accountability, which will keep you on the path to building wealth.

Rate of Return

One last note. We've already discussed how this growth compares to the growth of other investments, but I advise you not to get caught up in the returns. This is a platform to improve and enhance all your financial decisions. To compare the returns directly to other investments would be a complete misunderstanding of what I'm trying to portray. I'm not suggesting this as a replacement for good investment opportunities but rather a better place to store and access cash for those investment opportunities. You can have the best of both worlds in this scenario.

The goal for many will be to find a better opportunity to grow their money and get better returns. That is great and admirable. Using cash value life insurance will not inhibit your ability to do so. Rather, it will make those opportunities even more profitable (See "But I Can Get a Higher Return").

Case Study 2

Lump Sum Contributions
Plus Ongoing Savings

This is the second case study and it's slightly different from the first one.

When life insurance is sold, many people are under the impression that they can't put in lump sums of money into their policy but have to pay the same premium for life. Since we've already discussed some of these items in previous chapters, the purpose of this case study is to show you how efficient it is to put large sums of money quickly into a life insurance policy. I'm going to illustrate the following:

- Initial lump sum of $150,000 divided into two payments of $75,000 each.
- Annual contribution of $20,000 after year two.
- Total cash value at the end of every year.
- Total death benefit at the end of every year.
- Future income from the policy.

The same statement applies here. These numbers are examples

and not the rule. They can be altered significantly depending on your circumstances.

Year	Age End Year	Annual Outlay Beg Year	Net Cash Value End Year	Net Death Benefit End Year
40 Year Old Male, Good Health, Non-Smoker				
1	41	75,000	71,834	1,892,256
2	42	75,000	148,889	2,098,007
3	43	20,000	176,003	2,126,567
4	44	20,000	203,577	2,152,987
5	45	20,000	231,600	2,177,595
6	46	20,000	258,671	2,195,894
7	47	20,000	287,258	2,216,106
8	48	20,000	318,271	1,800,770
9	49	20,000	351,200	1,827,249
10	50	20,000	386,137	1,855,599
11	51	20,000	423,251	1,886,104
12	52	20,000	462,565	1,918,746
13	53	20,000	504,252	1,953,887
14	54	20,000	548,398	1,991,574
15	55	20,000	595,186	2,032,186
16	56	20,000	645,457	2,077,604
17	57	20,000	699,334	2,127,636
18	58	20,000	757,100	2,182,462
19	59	20,000	818,923	2,241,396
20	60	20,000	884,999	2,304,520
21	61	20,000	955,470	2,370,604
22	62	20,000	1,029,915	2,440,155
23	63	20,000	1,108,482	2,513,542
24	64	20,000	1,191,305	2,590,911
25	65	20,000	1,278,608	2,672,259
26	66	20,000	1,370,494	2,757,395
27	67	20,000	1,467,320	2,846,449
28	68	20,000	1,569,269	2,939,046
29	69	20,000	1,676,592	3,035,348

By splitting the lump sum into two contributions, we maximize its efficiency. While we are still slightly behind in year one, we see positive growth in year three. Just like any other investment, since we are putting more money in upfront, the money is working for us sooner, and it takes less time to become highly efficient.

While we see similar returns in Case Studies 1 and 2, around 5%, there is more capital working, and it becomes more efficient quicker, with more cash value and more death benefit.

Backdating the Policy
In many cases, cash value life insurance policies can be "backdated" to increase the ability to get money in quicker. For example, in the case above, we are splitting $150,000 into 2 contributions. If we start the policy on January 1st, the next premium contribution will be on January 1st of the following year.

In some cases, you would like to get that money in faster than in one year. Backdating the policy is a way to speed up that process. Instead of the policy being effective on January 1st, oftentimes insurance companies will allow that effective date to be up to six months sooner. In this case, the policy's effective date is July 1st of the previous year. By doing so, the policy's anniversary date would be technically six months later or the following July 1st. This puts the lump sum into the policy in the span of six months as opposed to a full year.

40 Year Old Male, Good Health, Non-Smoker

Year	Age End Year	Annual Outlay Beg Year	Net Cash Value End Year	Net Death Benefit End Year
30	70	0	1,767,335	2,865,237
31	71	0	1,862,731	2,949,739
32	72	0	1,962,891	3,037,449
33	73	0	2,068,053	3,129,478
34	74	0	2,178,488	3,225,765
35	75	0	2,294,296	3,326,127
36	76	-160,000	2,247,161	3,191,356
37	77	-160,000	2,196,789	3,057,848
38	78	-160,000	2,143,128	2,925,691
39	79	-160,000	2,086,127	2,815,120
40	80	-160,000	2,025,576	2,716,252
41	81	-160,000	1,961,330	2,624,241
42	82	-160,000	1,892,954	2,540,316
43	83	-160,000	1,820,096	2,451,531
44	84	-160,000	1,742,367	2,357,437
45	85	-160,000	1,659,306	2,257,583
46	86	-160,000	1,570,761	2,152,249
47	87	-160,000	1,476,276	2,041,292
48	88	-160,000	1,374,608	1,923,480
49	89	-160,000	1,264,992	1,798,112
50	90	-160,000	1,146,614	1,664,367
51	91	-160,000	1,018,758	1,521,366
52	92	-160,000	881,112	1,367,282
53	93	-160,000	733,147	1,200,956
54	94	-160,000	574,601	1,021,059
55	95	0	573,466	994,065
56	96	0	570,811	958,428
57	97	0	570,249	911,532
58	98	0	576,400	849,564
59	99	0	597,872	766,229

The second half of this case study shows the difference in retirement income when putting more money in upfront. In this scenario, we're seeing an increase from $120,000 per year of income to $160,000. Simply put, the more you put in, and the faster it gets there, the better the long-term growth.

Summary

Case Study 2: Lump Sum Contribution Plus Ongoing Savings	
Total Contributions	$690,000
Total Income	$3,040,000

Case Study 3

Lump Sum Only

This last case study illustrates the ability to drop in cash immediately, without worrying about ongoing savings. While we've talked about flexibility and the fact that you don't have to pay premiums your entire life, this case study exemplifies that reality.

Here's what I'm going to show you:

- Initial lump sum of $150,000 divided into two payments of $75,000 each.
- No annual contribution.
- Total cash value at the end of every year.
- Total death benefit at the end of every year.

40 Year Old Male, Good Health, Non-Smoker

Year	Age End Year	Annual Outlay Beg Year	Net Cash Value End Year	Net Death Benefit End Year
1	41	75,000	72,052	1,867,850
2	42	75,000	149,182	2,085,198
3	43	0	155,462	2,046,667
4	44	0	161,089	2,006,787
5	45	0	165,993	1,965,740
6	46	0	168,902	1,919,539
7	47	0	171,816	1,874,995
8	48	0	175,837	1,235,411
9	49	0	180,151	1,197,544
10	50	0	184,766	1,161,400
11	51	0	195,274	540,506
12	52	0	206,375	553,137
13	53	0	218,101	566,216
14	54	0	230,477	579,773
15	55	0	243,550	593,909
16	56	0	257,364	608,727
17	57	0	271,955	624,195
18	58	0	287,370	640,378
19	59	0	303,653	657,130
20	60	0	320,835	674,477
21	61	0	338,953	692,475
22	62	0	358,058	711,264
23	63	0	378,182	730,942
24	64	0	399,362	751,556
25	65	0	421,665	773,116
26	66	0	445,098	795,572
27	67	0	469,751	818,952
28	68	0	495,681	843,181
29	69	0	522,932	868,283
30	70	0	551,567	894,211
31	71	0	581,652	921,079
32	72	0	613,207	948,899
33	73	0	646,309	978,026
34	74	0	681,027	1,008,420
35	75	0	717,397	1,040,038

40 Year Old Male, Good Health, Non-Smoker

Year	Age End Year	Annual Outlay Beg Year	Net Cash Value End Year	Net Death Benefit End Year
36	76	0	755,475	1,072,904
37	77	0	795,119	1,106,777
38	78	0	836,336	1,141,724
39	79	0	879,075	1,177,832
40	80	0	923,311	1,215,202
41	81	0	969,114	1,253,915
42	82	0	1,016,494	1,294,139
43	83	0	1,065,446	1,335,731
44	84	0	1,115,982	1,378,692
45	85	0	1,168,088	1,423,023
46	86	0	1,222,180	1,469,391
47	87	0	1,278,290	1,517,961
48	88	0	1,335,734	1,567,984
49	89	0	1,394,393	1,619,373
50	90	0	1,454,178	1,672,045
51	91	0	1,515,041	1,725,893
52	92	0	1,577,192	1,780,508
53	93	0	1,640,726	1,835,737
54	94	0	1,705,907	1,891,417
55	95	0	1,773,148	1,947,359
56	96	0	1,843,235	2,003,299
57	97	0	1,918,325	2,058,885
58	98	0	2,000,935	2,113,210
59	99	0	2,095,554	2,164,672
60	100	0	2,210,600	2,210,600

In this illustration, we have successfully dropped a full lump sum of $150,000 into the policy without contributing another dollar. As you can see, the policy requires no more contributions and maintains its growth.

This is a great way to illustrate the flexibility of these policies when structured appropriately.

CHAPTER 11

WHAT'S NEXT?

In this book we've covered start to finish why the wealthy use life insurance as a tax free savings vehicle, but we haven't gotten extremely practical just yet on how you move forward if you would like to begin utilizing this strategy for you and your family. There's nothing that would disappoint me more than for you to read this book and then execute poorly because you didn't know where to look or the right questions to ask.

First, some expectations. You will need to work with a licensed insurance agent that can set up a high cash value policy for you. There is no other option. To find the right agent, you'll want to focus on the merging of two scales: Trust and Competence.

	Competent	Not Competent
Trustworthy	x	
Not Trustworthy		

You need to find someone that you can trust and also has the skill set and know-how to design a life insurance policy for high amounts of cash value. Trust is more difficult because it's less tangible, but you know it in your gut. You need to feel like you are working with someone who has your best interest in mind, not their own, because there is a real tradeoff between the commissions an insurance agent makes and the value given to a client (unfortunately).

By way of competency, scrub their knowledge against the content of this book, and use the example case studies as your guide (with some flexibility as a competent agent will be able to help you see why the numbers can adjust based on circumstances).

A competent agent will also recommend a highly rated mutual insurance company that has a strong reputation for financial strength and stability. You can easily find the rating of an insurance company by doing a quick Google search with the insurance company's name followed by "credit rating." You'll want the highest rating possible, minimum of an A rating.

There are 4 mutual insurance companies that are referred to as the "major mutual companies." They are MassMutual, Guardian, New York Life, and Northwestern Mutual, and they are all good options to consider. Just keep in mind that most agents who work for these companies will not know how to design a policy for high cash value, so you are looking for agent competency first, not insurance company first. If an agent gave you this book, that's a strong indicator they know what they are doing. I'll also offer a way to get a second opinion below if you are in the process and just want to be sure it's set up properly for high cash value.

CHAPTER 12

MY FINAL WORDS

It's an unfortunate reality that many of the citizens of the wealthiest country in the world are struggling financially. We are overspending, leveraging excessive amounts of credit, and struggling to make wise investment decisions. We've followed the unfortunate belief that the markets are the best way to save for the future, that locking money into government plans is smart, and that Wall Street advisors will not let you down.

I hope this book has effectively brought you back to our roots. I hope it has helped you see that you don't need to take risks to create a strong, stable financial foundation, and that there are better options out there than what you may have always known.

Cash value life insurance is a powerful financial tool that can put you back on the path to real wealth. It has been used by wealthy Americans, big banks, and large corporations for centuries and has stood strong through some of the most difficult financial times in history.

It is one of the least understood financial tools we have and the most underutilized one by the average American.

While not everyone is in the right situation to take advantage of the benefits inside a cash value life insurance policy, I truly believe it is the best place to build a strong financial foundation.Its benefits are unparalleled, and it gives you complete and total control of your own financial future.

I have personally found sincere satisfaction in putting these strategies into practice in my own life.

Thank you for taking the time to read this book. I hope this information will be as beneficial to you as it has been to me.

If you would like to discuss more about how we can help, feel free to reach out to whoever gave you this book or sign up for a free financial analysis here:

Get a second look or schedule a financial analysis. Scan the QR code or follow the link:

WealthbyJake.com/mwli4

For Financial Professionals

Are you an insurance agent or financial advisor wanting to purchase books in bulk, book me at an event, or learn how to offer these strategies to your clients? Learn how to work with me by scanning the QR code below or follow the link:

WealthbyJake.com/agent

ABOUT THE AUTHOR

Jake Thompson's work has helped thousands of individuals, families, and business owners use cash value life insurance to build wealth and find financial peace of mind. He is also very passionate about learning and growth and is the founder of Heroes Academy, a leading K-12 in the reinventing of traditional education.

Contact Information

Jake Thompson
WealthbyJake.com
Jake@WealthbyJake.com

For a compilation of all the references in this book or to contact me, scan the QR code or follow the link:

WealthbyJake.com/mwli1

Made in United States
Orlando, FL
08 January 2024

42242977R00046